RESCUING Animals FROM DISASTERS

SAVING ANIMALS FROM OIL SPILLS

by **Stephen Person**

Consultant: Michael A. Seymour
Louisiana Department of Wildlife and Fisheries

BEARPORT PUBLISHING

New York, New York

Credits

Cover and Title Page, © AP Photo/Charlie Riedel; 4, © Win McNamee/Getty Images; 5, © AP Photo/Charlie Riedel; 6, © Saul Loeb/AFP/Getty Images; 7L, © AP Photo/Chuck Cook; 7R, © Exactostock/SuperStock; 8L, © AFP/Getty Images/Newscom; 8R, © Lightroom Photos/USCG/Redux; 10, © AP Photo/Charlie Neibergall; 11L, © AP Photo/Charlie Riedel; 11R, © AP Photo/Kerry Sanders/NBC NewsWire; 12, © AP Photo/Charlie Riedel; 13T, © Sean Gardner/Reuters/Landov; 13B, © AP Photo/Charlie Neibergall; 14, © Carolyn Cole/Los Angeles Times; 15, Courtesy of University of California, Davis. Deepwater Horizon Response; 16, © Barbara Bergwerf/bergwerfgraphics.com; 17T, Courtesy of U.S. Fish and Wildlife Service/Bonnie Strawser; 17B, © AP Photo/Dave Martin; 18, © IBRRC; 19, © Jordan Rae Lake/IBRRC; 20, © AP Photo; 21T, © Alissa Crandall/AlaskaStock; 21B, © AP Photo; 22, © KOMO 4 News; 23, © Rachel Nixon; 24L, © Chris Arend/Alaska Stock LLC/Alamy; 24R, © Minden Pictures/SuperStock; 25, © AP Photo/Dave Martin; 26, Courtesy of U.S. Coast Guard/Petty Officer 3rd Class Robert Brazzell; 27, © AP Photo/Phil Sandlin; 28, © Martin Harvey/Photo Researchers, Inc.; 29, © Hirose/e-Photography/SeaPics; 31, © Leo Francini/Shutterstock; 32, Courtesy of U.S. Fish and Wildlife Service/Kim Betton.

Publisher: Kenn Goin
Editorial Director: Adam Siegel
Creative Director: Spencer Brinker
Design: Dawn Beard Creative and Kim Jones
Photo Researcher: James O'Connor

Library of Congress Cataloging-in-Publication Data

Person, Stephen.
  Saving animals from oil spills / by Stephen Person.
      p. cm. — (Rescuing animals from disasters)
  Includes bibliographical references and index.
  ISBN-13: 978-1-61772-288-2 (library binding)
  ISBN-10: 1-61772-288-X (library binding)
  1. Animal rescue—Juvenile literature. 2. Oil spills—Juvenile literature. 3. Oil pollution of water—Juvenile literature. I. Title.
  QL83.2.P48 2012
  628.1'6833—dc22
                                    2011002430

For more information, write to Bearport Publishing Company, Inc., 45 West 21st Street, Suite 3B, New York, New York 10010. Printed in the United States of America in North Mankato, Minnesota.

070111
042711CGA

10 9 8 7 6 5 4 3 2 1

CONTENTS

Kayla to the Rescue

On June 5, 2010, Kayla DiBenedetto (dee-*ben*-uh-DET-oh) sat in a small boat off the coast of Grand Isle, Louisiana. She lifted a pair of binoculars to her eyes and pointed them at the beach. She saw what she was looking for—pelicans. Many of the birds were covered with sticky brown oil. She knew that without quick help, they could die.

Birds covered with oil are called "oiled birds." Some of the birds that Kayla saw, like this pelican, were covered in so much oil that they could not move.

Kayla grabbed a large net and stepped out of the boat. She splashed through shallow water toward the oil-covered birds. "Our job was to capture them safely—not an easy task," she said. As Kayla got close, the frightened pelicans ran away. Kayla chased after them, but she tripped and fell facedown in the sand. She was not about to give up, though. Kayla was **determined** to save the birds.

Kayla's white suit helped protect her from the oil that was on the birds and in the water.

Kayla works for the U.S. Fish and Wildlife Service, a government group that protects animals and their **habitats**.

Racing to the Coast

Kayla is a **biologist** who works in Louisiana. On most days, her job is to study fish in Louisiana's waters. In the spring of 2010, however, she learned that an oil spill was spreading across the Gulf of Mexico. She knew this accident could be deadly for animals living around the Gulf. Like many scientists, Kayla left her regular job, raced to the coast, and joined a wildlife rescue team.

This biologist is rescuing a pelican that was covered in oil from the spill in the Gulf of Mexico.

Pelicans and other **seabirds** are wild animals and are not used to being handled by people. As a result, they get very nervous when they are captured. Rescuers must handle the animals very gently, because **stress** can kill birds.

Though it wasn't easy, Kayla managed to catch many oiled pelicans. She brought the birds by boat to rescue centers along the coast, where they could be cleaned. Kayla then turned her boat around and went back to look for more birds in trouble. "We didn't stop as long as there were still things to do," Kayla said. "We were trying to help every bird."

Oiled birds were kept in small cages until they could be brought to rescue centers.

Explosion in the Gulf

What disaster brought Kayla and others racing to the Gulf of Mexico? That story begins on the Deepwater Horizon—an **oil rig** that was 42 miles (68 km) off the coast of Louisiana in April 2010. Workers were using the rig's drill to reach oil in the rocks beneath the Gulf of Mexico. A long pipe carried oil up from the **well** to the rig. Suddenly, on April 20, gas that had built up in the well's pipe caused an explosion that shook the oil rig.

The Deepwater Horizon oil rig before the explosion

After the explosion, fire spread across the oil rig. Special firefighting ships tried to put out the flames, but they could not save the rig.

The blast killed 11 workers and caused the Deepwater Horizon to sink. As the rig sank, the pipe carrying oil up from the well cracked. Oil then flowed out of the broken pipe and into the Gulf of Mexico. Workers tried their best to seal the leak—but it wasn't easy. Oil continued to gush out of the pipe for nearly three months!

Oil in the Gulf

This map shows how far the oil spread in the Gulf of Mexico in just 10 days.

By the time workers had stopped the oil leak in July, more than 200 million gallons (757 million liters) of oil had flowed into the Gulf, making it the largest oil spill ever in U.S. waters.

Oil and Wildlife

As much as two and a half million gallons (9.4 million liters) of oil flowed from the broken pipe into the Gulf of Mexico every day. Scientists knew that the Gulf's wildlife was in serious danger. They were especially worried about pelicans and other seabirds. Why?

Pelicans can come on shore to get away from oil in water. However, since the birds feed on fish, they have to return to the oily water or they will starve to death.

Seabirds spend much of their life in water. To keep their bodies warm and dry, they are covered with feathers that act like a **waterproof** coat. When oil gets on a seabird's feathers, however, they stick together. Cold water and air are then able to reach the bird's skin. As a result, the bird can get too cold and may suffer from **hypothermia**, which can be deadly.

This bird's feathers are covered with so much oil that they can no longer keep the bird's body warm and dry.

Pelicans and other animals can be poisoned by eating oil-covered fish. Scientists from the Louisiana Department of Wildlife and Fisheries found this dead dolphin in the Gulf. It may have died from oil poisoning.

Cleaning Oiled Birds

Oiled birds must be cleaned quickly or they can die. After the Gulf spill, **veterinarians** and other trained workers set up rescue centers along the Gulf Coast. At these centers, the birds were taken inside warm buildings and fed. Workers washed each oiled bird in a tub using hot water and liquid soap. Clean birds were then taken to a second tub, where the soap was rinsed off.

This oiled pelican was cleaned at a rescue center in Buras, Louisiana.

Once they were cleaned and rinsed, the birds were placed in outdoor pools. Nets above the pools kept the birds from flying away. Veterinarians kept a close watch on the birds for several days. Healthy birds were released into clean areas of the Gulf as soon as possible—usually after about seven days.

Pelicans before—and after—they were cleaned

It took rescue workers about 45 minutes to clean each bird. They used up to 300 gallons (1,136 l) of water on each one.

Turtle Patrol

The oil that was spilling into the Gulf was also a danger to sea turtles. Sea turtles come to the water's surface to feed on floating **algae**. If they swallow oil along with the algae, the oil can damage their **organs** and kill them. Early each morning, scientists **patrolled** the Gulf in search of oiled turtles. The turtles they found were rushed to rescue centers to be cleaned.

Scientists used nets to scoop oiled turtles out of the water.

One of the many turtles saved was a young Kemp's ridley turtle nicknamed Lucky by rescue workers. Michele Kelley of the Audubon Nature Institute in Louisiana helped clean Lucky—but it wasn't easy. He was so small she had to use a toothbrush to get the oil out of the folds in his skin.

Workers had to use toothbrushes to clean Lucky and other young turtles.

Oiled turtles were fed mayonnaise. As the mayonnaise moved through each one's **digestive system**, it helped clean out the oil the turtle had swallowed.

The Great Egg Rescue

While scientists were saving oiled turtles, they realized that baby turtles, called **hatchlings**, were in danger as well. Sea turtles lay their eggs on the beach. When hatchlings come out of the eggs, they crawl down to the water and swim out to sea. If they did this during the Gulf oil spill, they would be entering oily waters and might not survive.

Tiny turtle hatchlings crawling down the beach to the ocean

To save baby turtles from getting covered with oil, scientists came up with a bold plan. They carefully dug up more than 28,000 sea turtle eggs from Gulf beaches. Then they packed the **delicate** eggs in boxes and took them by truck to the Atlantic coast of Florida. The eggs were kept in a warm building until they hatched in summer. The baby turtles were then released on clean Florida beaches, where they crawled into the Atlantic Ocean—safe from the Gulf oil spill.

A nest of sea turtle eggs

Of the 28,000 eggs that were moved, about 15,000 hatchlings made it to the ocean. This is a very high success rate. In nature, animals such as raccoons and birds eat more than half of all turtle eggs and hatchlings before they can reach the water.

The turtle eggs were packed in sand and kept warm in foam boxes. They were moved nearly 500 miles (805 km) so that they would be near a clean beach when they hatched.

Wildlife Hero

What makes a person want to spend his or her life rescuing animals from oil spills? Wildlife rescuer Jay Holcomb can answer that question. "As a kid of nine or ten, I just knew I was going to take care of wildlife," Jay said.

Jay has been saving birds from oil spills since the early 1970s.

In 1971, when Jay was in his early 20s, he heard that oil was spilling from a ship in California's San Francisco Bay. He rushed to the bay and helped pull thousands of birds from the oily water. At that time, no one knew how to clean the birds, however, and nearly all of them died. "It was horrible," said Jay. After that, he decided to learn everything he could about how to care for oiled wildlife.

Jay (left) helps care for an injured bird.

Today, Jay is one of the world's top experts in rescuing oiled wildlife. For 25 years, he helped lead the International Bird Rescue Research Center, based in California. During the Gulf spill, Jay led a team of 88 trained rescuers to the Gulf.

Disaster in Alaska

Jay has worked at more than 200 oil spills around the world. One of the worst ones happened in Alaska in 1989. An oil **tanker** named the *Exxon Valdez* smashed into a rocky **reef**. The ship's **hull** ripped open, spilling about 11 million gallons (42 million liters) of oil into Prince William Sound. Oil soon covered many animals that lived in the water, including thousands of sea otters.

The *Exxon Valdez* before the accident

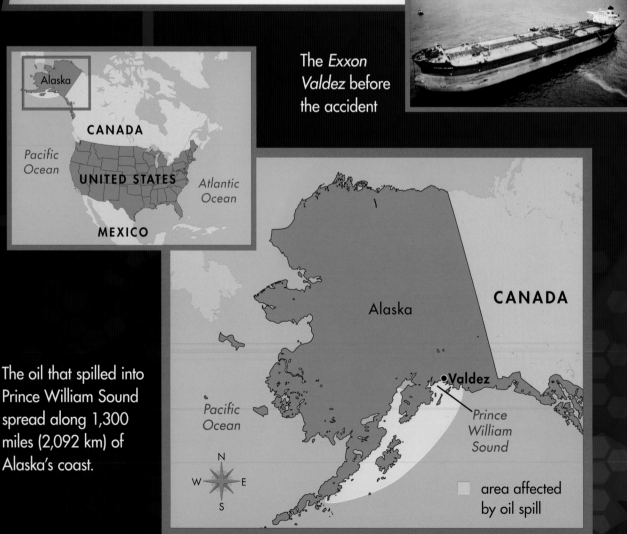

The oil that spilled into Prince William Sound spread along 1,300 miles (2,092 km) of Alaska's coast.

The oiled otters were in need of quick help. Sea otters have fur that keeps their bodies warm in the cold ocean. When fur gets covered with oil, it doesn't **insulate** the animals very well, and otters can freeze to death. In addition, otters try to clean off the oil by licking their fur. This is deadly, because they swallow the oil, which poisons them. Animal rescue workers in Alaska helped clean more than 300 oiled otters.

Workers wash oil off this sea otter.

During the *Exxon Valdez* spill, about 2,800 sea otters died before rescuers could help them. The oil spill also killed around 250,000 seabirds, 300 seals, 22 killer whales, and billions of fish eggs.

This seabird was covered in oil during the *Exxon Valdez* spill.

Learning from Nuka

When the sea otters in Alaska were clean and in good health again, they were released back into the wild. Some otters, however, were too small or weak to survive on their own. One of these was a baby otter, which rescue workers named Nuka. So that she would have a safe home, Nuka was sent to live at the Seattle Aquarium in Seattle, Washington.

Nuka was born during the *Exxon Valdez* oil spill and could not have survived in Prince William Sound.

Nuka died in 2010, at the age of 21. In the wild, sea otters usually live only 10 to 15 years, because animals, such as great white sharks and killer whales, often eat them.

By studying Nuka, scientists were able to learn more about the long-term effects of oil on animals. For example, Nuka had many health problems, including skin diseases and a weak **immune system**. Scientists believe that the oil that got into her body after she tried to lick it off her fur caused these problems.

Nyac was another baby otter rescued during the *Exxon Valdez* spill. She lived nearly 20 years at the Vancouver Aquarium in Canada.

Lasting Dangers

The *Exxon Valdez* spill taught scientists another lesson—oil spills can be deadly long after the oil stops spilling. For example, oil can enter the **food chain** and be passed from one living thing to another. After the *Exxon Valdez* spill, oil covered clams, crabs, and mussels. When birds and otters ate the shellfish, the oil got into their bodies and made them sick.

Otters depend on crabs and other sea creatures for their food.

Scientists believe that after the *Exxon Valdez* oil spill, many killer whales were poisoned by eating oiled fish and seals.

What long-term effects will the Gulf oil spill of 2010 have on wildlife? Scientists will be studying that for many years to come. The good news is that on July 15, 2010, workers were able to place a cap over the broken oil pipe. After 87 days, oil finally stopped flowing into the Gulf of Mexico.

In the six months after the Gulf spill began, workers cleaned more than two million pounds (907,185 kg) of oiled debris from beaches and wetlands along the Gulf.

Workers clean oil off the beaches along the Gulf of Mexico. Oil on beaches can continue to harm wildlife long after it is spilled.

Back to the Wild

By October 2010, more than five months after the Deepwater Horizon exploded, there were signs that the Gulf was beginning to **recover** from the oil spill. Scientists tested water off the Louisiana coast. It was clean enough for sea turtles to swim and feed safely. Scientists carried 32 sea turtles onto small motorboats. These turtles had been rescued from the oily waters. Now it was time for them to go home.

Rescuers release pelicans back into the wild.

By October 2010, wildlife rescuers in the Gulf had cleaned and released more than 1,200 birds. All the bird rescue centers built to respond to the Gulf oil spill were closed by November 2010.

"Let's go free some turtles, people!" shouted one of the scientists. The boats carried the turtles to their home waters, 50 miles (80 km) off the coast. There, scientists picked up the turtles, lowered them into the clean water, and watched them swim away. The rescuers' work was finally done.

During the oil spill, rescue workers pulled about 500 oiled sea turtles from the Gulf. Some of these turtles later died, possibly from oil they had eaten. However, more than 360 were cleaned and returned to the Gulf by the end of 2010.

FAMOUS OIL SPILLS AND RESCUES

Rescue workers have learned a lot from working at oil spills all over the world. Here are two major spills that put wildlife in danger.

Ixtoc I Well Spill, Gulf of Mexico, 1979

- On June 3, 1979, an oil rig that had been digging a well off the coast of Mexico exploded. About 140 million gallons (530 million liters) of oil from the damaged well gushed into the Gulf of Mexico over the following 290 days.

- Oil covered many beaches along the eastern coast of Mexico. It killed up to 10,000 birds as well as many fish, shrimp, and squid.

- Oil in the water and on the beaches also put sea turtles in danger. The United States and Mexico worked together to catch turtles and take them by airplane to areas of the Gulf that were clean.

This penguin was covered in oil from the *Treasure* spill.

Treasure *Spill, South Africa, 2000*

- On June 23, 2000, the oil ship *Treasure* sank off the coast of South Africa. About 1,300 tons (1,179 metric tons) of oil spilled from the ship.

- One of the world's largest populations of African penguins lives on islands near the spill. More than 20,000 of the penguins became covered with oil.

- Experts from the International Bird Rescue Research Center worked with local rescue workers to help the birds. More than 18,000 of the oiled birds were cleaned and released back into the wild. At that time, it was the largest seabird rescue in history.

ANIMALS AT RISK FROM SPILLS

Oil spills are dangerous to many kinds of wildlife. When oil gets in the water, it harms different kinds of wildlife in different ways.

Marine Mammals

- **Marine mammals** include sea otters, seals, dolphins, and whales.
- Oil spills can harm their skin by causing painful burns and rashes.
- Marine mammals may eat fish or shellfish that have taken in oil. As a result, the food marine mammals eat after a spill can poison them.
- Marine mammals need to come to the water's surface to breathe air. During an oil spill, they may breathe in **toxic fumes** rising from the oily water. These fumes can damage their **lungs**—and even kill them.

Fish

- While swimming through water after a spill, fish may take in oil through their skin or mouths. This oil may damage their organs, causing the fish to have weaker immune systems. As a result, it will be harder for them to fight off diseases.
- Fish eggs and **larvae** can be killed by oil. When this happens, the population of that fish may drop rapidly.
- The Gulf spill was dangerous to bluefin tuna, sharks, and other fish. In the years to come, scientists will watch for changes in the populations of these fish.

Bluefin tuna are at risk from oil spills such as the one in the Gulf of Mexico in 2010.

GLOSSARY

algae (AL-jee) small plant-like organisms that grow in water or on damp surfaces

biologist (bye-OL-uh-jist) a scientist who studies plants or animals

debris (duh-BREE) scattered pieces of something that has been wrecked or destroyed

delicate (DEL-uh-kuht) easily hurt

determined (di-TUR-mind) having a strong will to do something

digestive system (dye-JESS-tiv SISS-tuhm) the group of organs in people or animals that help break down food so the body can use it for fuel

food chain (FOOD CHAYN) a series of plants and animals that depend on one another for food

habitats (HAB-uh-*tats*) places in nature where a plant or animal normally lives

hatchlings (HACH-lingz) animals that have recently come out of eggs

hull (HUHL) the frame or body of a ship

hypothermia (*hye*-puh-THUR-mee-uh) a condition in which a person's or animal's body temperature becomes dangerously low

immune system (i-MYOON SISS-tuhm) the system that a body uses to protect itself from harmful germs that can cause diseases

insulate (IN-suh-*layt*) to protect something from losing heat, usually by surrounding it with some kind of material

larvae (LAR-vee) the young form of some animals, such as fish, when they are just born or hatched from eggs

lungs (LUHNGZ) the body parts a person or animal uses for breathing air

marine mammals (muh-REEN MAM-uhlz) warm-blooded animals that live in the ocean, have hair or fur on their skin, and drink their mothers' milk as babies

oil rig (OIL RIG) an offshore platform used to drill for oil beneath the ocean floor

organs (OR-guhnz) body parts, such as the lungs or heart, that do a particular job

patrolled (puh-TROHLD) traveled around an area to keep it safe

recover (ri-KOV-ur) to get better after a difficult period

reef (REEF) a ridge of rock, sand, or coral that lies near the surface of a body of water

seabirds (SEE-burdz) birds that spend most of their life at sea

stress (STRESS) nervousness, worry

tanker (TANG-kur) a ship that carries liquids, such as oil

toxic fumes (TOK-sik FYOOMZ) harmful gas or smoke given off by chemicals or something that is burning

veterinarians (*vet*-ur-uh-NAIR-ee-uhnz) doctors who take care of animals

waterproof (WAW-tur-*proof*) able to prevent water from passing through

well (WEL) a deep hole that people dig to get oil, water, gas, or steam

wetlands (WET-*landz*) swampy areas near lakes and rivers

BIBLIOGRAPHY

International Bird Rescue (www.bird-rescue.org/)

National Wildlife Federation (www.nwf.org/Oil-Spill/Effects-on-Wildlife.aspx)

Restore the Gulf (www.restorethegulf.gov/)

READ MORE

Beech, Linda Ward. *The* Exxon Valdez's *Deadly Oil Spill (Code Red)*. New York: Bearport (2007).

Benoit, Peter. *The BP Oil Spill*. New York: Children's Press (2011).

Berger, Melvin. *Oil Spill!* Boston: Houghton Mifflin (1999).

Harris, Joan. *One Wing's Gift: Rescuing Alaska's Wild Birds*. Portland, OR: Alaska Northwest Books (2002).

Landau, Elaine. *Oil Spill! Disaster in the Gulf of Mexico*. Minneapolis, MN: Millbrook Press (2011).

Smith, Roland. *Sea Otter Rescue: The Aftermath of an Oil Spill*. New York: Puffin Books (1999).

LEARN MORE ONLINE

To learn more about rescuing animals from oil spills, visit
www.bearportpublishing.com/RescuingAnimalsfromDisasters

INDEX

ABOUT THE AUTHOR

Stephen Person has written many children's books about history, science, and the environment. He lives with his family in Saratoga Springs, New York.